BASIC RULES OF NUMBER

Answer Book

Stage 6

Folens Publishers

Introduction

Basic Rules of Number is a series of books that offers a variety of calculation and problem-solving activities that are designed to develop numeracy skills. It is not intended that these books be used in the classroom as a number scheme. They are ideal for supplementing any published scheme of work or any scheme of work implemented by the school.

While there is a natural progression of understanding within each of the books, and subsequently within the series as a whole, it is not suggested that the children work their way systematically through each of the activities. Rather, the activities should be selected to support the work being undertaken in the classroom at the time. Alternatively they could be used as revision activities at a later date to ensure that a particular concept has been understood.

The children should not enter the answers to the problems directly into their text books. Rather they should write the whole problem together with the answer in an exercise book or on to a sheet of paper. The children might also be required to show their workings out at the same time.

This book has answers handwritten alongside each problem. Answers are only given where there can only be one answer. Often there are activities that can result in more than one correct answer. For example, on page 41, Activity 1, the children are asked to write four facts about some numbers. There are several ways in which they can do this and so no definitive answer is given. Similarly, where the children are asked to complete a lengthy calculation or activity, such as Activity 1 on page 43, the various answers are not given.

Please note
For teachers of children aged four to seven, this series includes three attractively-illustrated photocopiable books.

© 1995 Folens Limited, on behalf of the author.
First published 1995 by Folens Limited, Dunstable and Dublin.
Folens Limited, Albert House, Apex Business Centre, Boscombe Road, Dunstable, LU5 4RL.

ISBN 1 85276 790 1

Printed in the EU.

Editors: Janet Swarbrick and Alison Millar

Layout artist: Suzanne Ward

Illustrations: Chris Roper

Cover design: Kim Ashby

Cover illustration: Karen Tushingham

Cover production: Design for Marketing, Ware

Numbers

I Fill in the missing numbers.

We will try these now!

(a) 4, 8, 12 , 16 , 20, 24 .

(b) 6, 12, 18, 24 , 30 , 36 , 42 , 48 .

(c) 3, 6, 9 , 12 , 15, 18, 21 , 24 .

(d) 5, 10, 15 , 20 , 25 , 30, 35, 40 .

---

2 Which number does not follow the pattern in each sequence?

(a) 2, 4, 6, 8, 10, (11) 12, 14.

(b) 6, 12, 18, (25) 30, 36, 42, 48.

(c) 24, 32, 40, (46) 56, 64, 72.

(d) 7, 14, 21, 28, 35, (44) 49, 56.

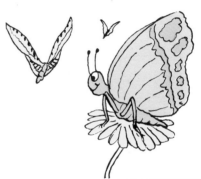

---

3 Write the missing numbers.

(a) 4 x 6 = 24

(b) 3 x 7 = 21

(c) 5 x 2 = 10

(d) 9 x 5 = 45

(e) 6 x 8 = 48

(f) 4 x 8 = 32

(g) 5 x 7 = 35

(h) 9 x 0 = 0

(i) 7 x 8 = 56

(j) 6 x 7 = 42

(k) 8 x 8 = 64

(l) 6 x 9 = 54

(m) 0 x 8 = 0

(n) 7 x 9 = 63

(o) 9 x 4 = 36

---

4 **(a)** There are 7 apples in a bag. How many are in 9 bags? 63

(b) There were 8 children at a party. They were given 6 balloons each. How many balloons were given out? 48

---

5 Copy the chart and fill in the missing numbers.

Number	4	6	9	7	6	8	9	6	9	8
Number	2	3	5	4	5	4	3	7	7	6
Product	8	18	45	28	30	32	27	42	63	48

Division

Division is the opposite of multiplication!

3 x 4 = 12	2 x 5 = 10	6 x 2 = 12
4 x 3 = 12	5 x 2 = 10	2 x 6 = 12
12 ÷ 4 = 3	10 ÷ 2 = 5	12 ÷ 2 = 6
12 ÷ 3 = 4	10 ÷ 5 = 2	12 ÷ 6 = 2

1 Write the missing numbers.

(a) 30 ÷ 6 = 5   (b) 15 ÷ 3 = 5   (c) 35 ÷ 7 = 5

(d) 36 ÷ 6 = 6   (e) 18 ÷ 3 = 6   (f) 42 ÷ 7 = 6

(g) 42 ÷ 6 = 7   (h) 21 ÷ 3 = 7   (i) 49 ÷ 7 = 7

(j) 48 ÷ 6 = 8   (k) 24 ÷ 3 = 8   (l) 56 ÷ 7 = 8

(m) 54 ÷ 6 = 9   (n) 3 ÷ 3 = 1   (o) 63 ÷ 7 = 9

2 How many 4s are in each of these numbers?

(a) 12   (b) 8   (c) 20   (d) 36
⓷   ②   ⑤   ⑨

(e) 16   (f) 32   (g) 24   (h) 28
④   ⑧   ⑥   ⑦

3 How many 9s in each of these?

(a) 9   (b) 27   (c) 63   (d) 81
①   ③   ⑦   ⑨

(e) 18   (f) 36   (g) 72   (h) 54
②   ④   ⑧   ⑥

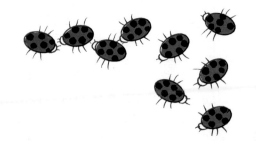

Time

1 Write the times shown on each clock face, first in words, then in figures.

half past nine	quarter to one	quarter past five	five to three	five past four
(a)	**(b)**	**(c)**	**(d)**	**(e)**

9·30   12·45   5·15   2·55   4·05

2 What time will each clock face show $\frac{1}{2}$ hour later?

(a) 10·00
(b) 1·15
(c) 5·45 (d) 3·25 (e) 4·35

3 What time did each clock face show 20 minutes earlier?

(a) 9·10
(b) 12·25
(c) 4·55 (d) 2·35 (e) 3·45

4 Write the missing numbers.

(a) How many minutes in 1 hour? ⑥⓪

(b) 2 hrs = [120] mins.

(c) $1\frac{1}{2}$ hrs = [90] mins.

(d) $2\frac{1}{4}$ hrs = [135] mins.

(e) 2 hrs 5 mins = [125] mins.

(f) 80 mins = [1] hrs [20] mins.

(g) 100 mins = [1] hrs [40] mins.

(h) How many seconds in 1 minute? [60]

(i) $1\frac{1}{2}$ mins = [90] seconds.

(j) $1\frac{1}{4}$ mins = [75] seconds.

(k) 130 secs = [2] mins [10] secs.

5 A watch shows 3.10am. It is 20 mins fast. Write the correct time. (2·50 am)

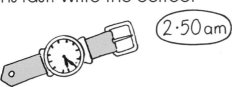

6 How many minutes from 1.20pm to 2.00pm? (40)

7 A TV show starts at 6.10pm and lasts for 55mins. At what time does it end?   7·05pm

8 Write the time that is 10 mins earlier than 5.05pm. (4·55 pm)

9 A cartoon on TV lasted 45 mins, the news report lasted 20 mins and the weather report lasted 3 mins. How long is that altogether? (1hr 8 mins)

Time–Addition and subtraction

Add	hrs mins
	1 35
	+ 2 45
	4 20

(80 mins = 1hr 20 mins)

Subtract	hrs mins	hrs mins
	4 10	3 70
	− 2 50	− 2 50
	1 20	1 20

(1 hr 10 mins = 60 mins + 10 mins)

Multiply	hrs mins	hrs mins
	35	2 20
	x 3	x 5
	1 45	11 40

(105 mins = 1hr 45 mins)

Divide	hrs mins	mins
	3) 4 15	3) 75
	1 25	25

(75 mins = 60 + 15 mins)

1

(a)
hrs	mins
2	30
+ 1	40
4	10

(b)
hrs	mins
3	20
+ 2	50
6	10

(c)
hrs	mins
4	25
+ 3	55
8	20

(d)
hrs	mins
2	45
+ 2	55
5	40

(e)
hrs	mins
1	40
2	25
+ 2	35
6	40

(f)
hrs	mins
2	35
1	15
+ 3	55
7	45

(g)
hrs	mins
2	18
1	27
+ 4	36
8	21

(h)
hrs	mins
3	36
2	29
+ 3	47
9	52

2

Alan was getting fit for the marathon. He jogged for 2 hrs 45 mins on Monday, 2 hrs 36 mins on Tuesday and 3 hrs 13 mins on Wednesday. How long did he jog on those 3 days? (8 hr 34mins)

3 Write the missing numbers.

(a)
hrs	mins
3	40
− 1	20
2	20

(b)
hrs	mins
4	20
− 1	40
2	40

(c)
hrs	mins
6	30
− 2	50
3	40

(d)
hrs	mins
5	40
− 1	50
3	50

(e)
hrs	mins
6	10
− 2	40
3	30

Basic Rules of Number: Stage 6

© Folens

Division

Example

There are 56 apples on the tree. Jim picked 14 apples on each visit to the tree. How many visits did he make to clear the apples from the tree?

$$
\begin{array}{r}
56 \\
-14 \\
\hline
42
\end{array} \rightarrow \text{visit 1}
$$

$$
\begin{array}{r}
-14 \\
\hline
28
\end{array} \rightarrow \text{visit 2}
$$

$$
\begin{array}{r}
-14 \\
\hline
14
\end{array} \rightarrow \text{visit 3}
$$

$$
\begin{array}{r}
-14 \\
\hline
0
\end{array} \rightarrow \text{visit 4}
$$

$$
\begin{array}{r}
4 \\
14\overline{)56} \\
-\ 56 \\
\hline
0
\end{array} \rightarrow 14 \times 4
$$

He will make 4 visits.

I Estimate then find the answers.

(a) $52 \div 13 = \boxed{4}$ (b) $60 \div 12 = \boxed{5}$ (c) $72 \div 12 = \boxed{6}$

(d) $17\overset{3}{\overline{)51}}$ (e) $13\overset{7}{\overline{)91}}$ (f) $14\overset{3}{\overline{)42}}$ (g) $16\overset{5}{\overline{)80}}$

(h) $18\overset{5}{\overline{)90}}$ (i) $19\overset{3}{\overline{)57}}$ (j) $14\overset{4}{\overline{)56}}$ (k) $12\overset{8}{\overline{)96}}$

(l) $13\overset{3\,r\,3}{\overline{)42}}$ (m) $15\overset{5\,r\,4}{\overline{)79}}$ (n) $13\overset{4\,r\,7}{\overline{)59}}$ (o) $12\overset{5\,r\,4}{\overline{)64}}$

---

2 98 players are put into 15-a-side teams.

(a) How many teams can be made? ⑥

(b) How many players cannot get into a team? ⑧

---

3 Bottles of cola are packed in boxes of 24.

How many boxes can be filled from 96 bottles? ③

(18 left over)

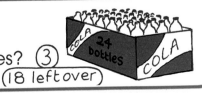

Division

Example

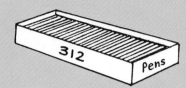

A teacher wants to divide the pens equally among 24 children.
How any pens will each child get?

Estimate (round up or down):

$$312 \rightarrow 300$$
$$24 \rightarrow 20$$

$$\begin{array}{r} 15 \\ 20\overline{)300} \end{array}$$

$$\left.\begin{array}{r} 13 \\ 24\overline{)312} \\ -\ 24 \\ \hline 72 \end{array}\right\} \rightarrow$$

Step 1 $31 \div 24 = 1$
Step 2 $24 \times 1 = 24$
Step 3   Subtract 24
Step 4   Put 2 alongside 7
Step 5 $72 \div 24 = 3$
Step 6 $24 \times 3 = 72$

Each child gets 13 pens.

---

1   Estimate the answers first.

(a) $17\overline{)272}^{\,16}$ (b) $14\overline{)210}^{\,15}$ (c) $18\overline{)252}^{\,14}$ (d) $13\overline{)299}^{\,23}$

(e) $13\overline{)159}^{\,12\,r3}$ (f) $17\overline{)229}^{\,13\,r8}$ (g) $23\overline{)391}^{\,17}$ (h) $23\overline{)414}^{\,18}$

(i) $17\overline{)236}^{\,13\,r15}$ (j) $19\overline{)254}^{\,13\,r7}$ (k) $23\overline{)607}^{\,26\,r9}$ (l) $21\overline{)540}^{\,25\,r15}$

(m) $23\overline{)294}^{\,12\,r18}$ (n) $25\overline{)601}^{\,24\,r1}$ (o) $31\overline{)710}^{\,22\,r28}$ (p) $33\overline{)649}^{\,19\,r22}$

---

2   37 times a certain number is 296. Find the number.   ⑧

3

These buses can each carry 46 people. 386 boys and 258 girls are going to a pop concert. How many buses are needed to get them there? ⑭

Division

Example

```
         245
    23)5635
    −  46      → 23 x 2
      103
     −92       → 23 x 4
      115
    −115       → 23 x 5
```

1

(a) $13\overline{)1599}$ → 123

(b) $17\overline{)2278}$ → 134

(c) $19\overline{)2755}$ → 145

(d) $21\overline{)4935}$ → 235

(e) $23\overline{)5658}$ → 246

(f) $23\overline{)5551}$ → 241 r 8

(g) $26\overline{)9101}$ → 350 r 1

(h) $29\overline{)4629}$ → 159 r 18

(i) $23\overline{)2438}$ → 106

(j) $19\overline{)2014}$ → 106

(k) $21\overline{)2247}$ → 107

(l) $26\overline{)5304}$ → 204

(m) $28\overline{)5796}$ → 207

(n) $29\overline{)5974}$ → 206

(o) $21\overline{)4389}$ → 209

(p) $31\overline{)9362}$ → 302

(q) $26\overline{)7904}$ → 304

(r) $23\overline{)7061}$ → 307

(s) $22\overline{)6776}$ → 308

(t) $19\overline{)7638}$ → 402

(u) $32\overline{)8891}$ → 277 r 27

(v) $41\overline{)8003}$ → 195 r 8

(w) $43\overline{)9702}$ → 225 r 27

(x) $47\overline{)5909}$ → 125 r 34

2 A boy delivered 4758 newspapers during the months of April and May.
He delivered the same number each day.

How many papers did he deliver daily? ⃝78

3 A gardener planted 1200 tulips, putting 37 tulips in each row.

(a) How many full rows will he have? (Estimate first.) ⃝32

(b) How many extra plants will he need to make another full row? ⃝21

Fractions

What fraction of each shape is
(**a**) shaded, (**b**) unshaded?

1 (a) $\frac{1}{4}$ (b) $\frac{3}{4}$

2 (a) $\frac{1}{3}$ (b) $\frac{2}{3}$

3 (a) $\frac{1}{6}$ (b) $\frac{5}{6}$

4 (a) $\frac{1}{10}$ (b) $\frac{9}{10}$
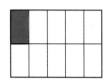

5 (a) $\frac{1}{8}$ (b) $\frac{7}{8}$

6 (a) $\frac{1}{5}$ (b) $\frac{4}{5}$
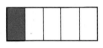

7 (a) $\frac{1}{9}$ (b) $\frac{8}{9}$
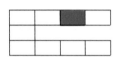

8 (a) $\frac{3}{8}$ (b) $\frac{5}{8}$

9 (a) $\frac{3}{10}$ (b) $\frac{7}{10}$
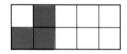

10 (a) $\frac{2}{5}$ (b) $\frac{3}{5}$

What fraction of each set is (**a**) black, (**b**) white?

11 (a) $\frac{1}{3}$ (b) $\frac{2}{3}$
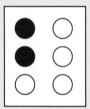

12 (a) $\frac{2}{5}$ (b) $\frac{3}{5}$
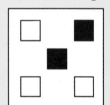

13 (a) 0 (b) 1 or $\frac{10}{10}$

14 (a) $\frac{4}{9}$ (b) $\frac{5}{9}$
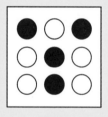

15 (a) $\frac{5}{12}$ (b) $\frac{7}{12}$
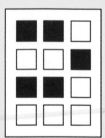

16 Find...

(**a**) $\frac{3}{4}$ of 32　(24)

(**b**) $\frac{3}{4}$ of 92　(69)

(**c**) $\frac{3}{4}$ of 108　(81)

(**d**) $\frac{3}{4}$ of 48　(36)

(**e**) $\frac{3}{4}$ of 60　(45)

(**f**) $\frac{3}{4}$ of 104　(78)

(**g**) $\frac{2}{3}$ of 78　(52)

(**h**) $\frac{2}{3}$ of 81　(54)

(**i**) $\frac{2}{3}$ of 144　(96)

(**j**) $\frac{5}{5}$ of 90　(90)

(**k**) $\frac{2}{5}$ of 145　(58)

(**l**) $\frac{3}{5}$ of 420　(252)

(**m**) $\frac{3}{8}$ of 60　(22$\frac{1}{2}$)

(**n**) $\frac{5}{6}$ of 90　(75)

(**o**) $\frac{5}{6}$ of 144　(120)

Decimals

Do you remember?

$\frac{1}{10}$ is shaded.

0.1 is shaded.

0.9 is **not** shaded.

$\frac{4}{10}$ or 0.4 is shaded.

$\frac{6}{10}$ = 0.$\boxed{6}$

1 What decimal fraction of each shape is shaded?

(a) 0·1

(b) 0·4

(c) 0·2

(d) 0·9

(e) 0·6

(f) 0·5

2 Write these fractions as decimals: (a) $\frac{2}{10}$ (b) $\frac{5}{10}$ (c) $\frac{8}{10}$ (d) $\frac{9}{10}$

(a) 0·2   (b) 0·5   (c) 0·8   (d) 0·9

3 Write these decimals as fractions: (a) 0.1   (b) 0.5   (c) 0.7   (d) 0.6

$\left(\frac{1}{10}\right)$ $\left(\frac{1}{2}\right)$ $\left(\frac{7}{10}\right)$ $\left(\frac{3}{5} \text{ or } \frac{6}{10}\right)$

4 Complete the number line.

(a) 0.4, 0.5, 0.6, $\boxed{0·7}$, $\boxed{0·8}$.   (b) 0.2, 0.4, $\boxed{0·6}$, $\boxed{0·8}$.

(c) 1.1, 1.3, 1.5, $\boxed{1·7}$, $\boxed{1·9}$.   (d) 2.4, 2.6, 2.8, $\boxed{3·0}$, $\boxed{3·2}$.

5 $\frac{1}{10}$ of my books is 9 books. How many books have I? (90)

6 0.1 of my books is 5 books. How many books have I? (50)

7 0.5 of a number is 12. What is the number? (24)

8 (a) 2.3 = 2 + $\frac{3}{10}$ (b) 10.5 = $\boxed{10}$ + $\boxed{\frac{5}{10}}$

(c) 1.7 = 1 + $\boxed{\frac{7}{10}}$ (d) 3 + $\frac{4}{10}$ = $\boxed{3·4}$

(e) 4.9 = $\boxed{4}$ + $\boxed{\frac{9}{10}}$ (f) 4 + $\frac{1}{2}$ = $\boxed{4·5}$

Decimals

This square is cut into 10 equal parts. $\frac{1}{10}$ or 0.1 is shaded.

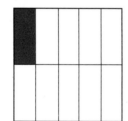

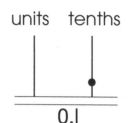

0.1

1

		true	false
(a) $1 + \frac{3}{10} = 1.3$		☑	☐
(c) $0.1 + \frac{2}{10} = 0.3$		☑	☐
(e) $\frac{9}{10} > \frac{4}{5}$		☑	☐

	true	false
(b) $\frac{1}{10} < 0.1$	☐	☑
(d) $2\frac{1}{2} = 2.2$	☐	☑
(f) 1.5 days = 1 day 5hrs	☐	☑

2 (a)
```
  1.6
+ 2.3
-----
  3·9
```
(b)
```
  2.4
+ 1.2
-----
  3·6
```
(c)
```
  3.2
+ 1.7
-----
  4·9
```
(d)
```
  2.5
+ 3.5
-----
  6·0
```

(e)
```
  5.7
- 1.3
-----
  4·4
```
(f)
```
  8.9
- 1.7
-----
  7·2
```
(g)
```
  3.2
- 1.7
-----
  1·5
```
(h)
```
  9.1
- 3.6
-----
  5·5
```

(i)
```
  5.6
+ 2.9
-----
  8·5
```
(j)
```
  7.0
- 1.4
-----
  5·6
```
(k)
```
  1.8
+ 1.8
-----
  3·6
```
(l)
```
 10.3
+ 1.7
-----
 12·0
```

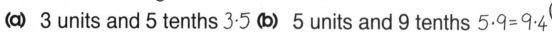

3 Write the following as decimals and add them.

(a) 3 units and 5 tenths 3·5 **(b)** 5 units and 9 tenths 5·9 = 9·4

(c) 2 units and a half. 2·5 **(d)** 1 unit and a half and 3 tenths
1·8 = 4·3

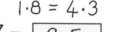

4 (a) $0.7 + 1.9 + 8 =$ 10·6 **(b)** $5 + 0.8 + 3.7 =$ 9·5

5 One twin saved 90 stamps for his collection.
The other twin only saved 0.7 of that.
How many stamps did they save altogether? (153)

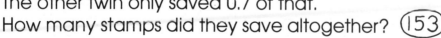

Decimals

This square is cut into 100 equal parts.
$\frac{1}{100}$ is shaded.

$\frac{1}{100}$ can be written 0.01 (zero point zero one).

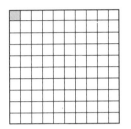

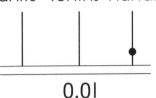

0.01

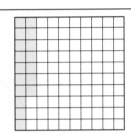

17 hundredths are shaded.

$\frac{17}{100}$ or 0.17 is shaded.

$\frac{83}{100}$ or 0.83 is **not** shaded.

What decimal fraction of each of these shapes is
(**a**) shaded, (**b**) unshaded?

1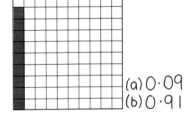
(a) 0·09
(b) 0·91

2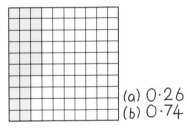
(a) 0·26
(b) 0·74

3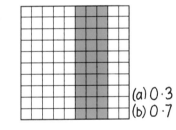
(a) 0·3
(b) 0·7

4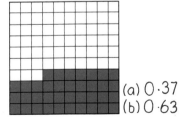
(a) 0·37
(b) 0·63

5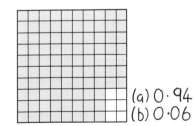
(a) 0·94
(b) 0·06

6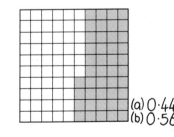
(a) 0·44
(b) 0·56

7

$$2.59 = 2 + \frac{5}{10} + \frac{9}{100}$$

Write the following numbers in the same way:

(**a**) 1.29
$1 + \frac{2}{10} + \frac{9}{100}$

(**b**) 3.76
$3 + \frac{7}{10} + \frac{6}{100}$

(**c**) 4.03
$4 + \frac{3}{100}$

(**d**) 7.09
$7 + \frac{9}{100}$

(**e**) 5.38
$5 + \frac{3}{10} + \frac{8}{100}$

(**f**) 3.01
$3 + \frac{1}{100}$

Basic Rules of Number: Stage 6

Decimals

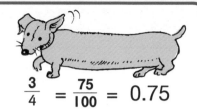

Important!

$\frac{1}{2} = \frac{5}{10} = 0.5$ $\qquad$ $\frac{1}{4} = \frac{25}{100} = 0.25$ $\qquad$ $\frac{3}{4} = \frac{75}{100} = 0.75$

1 Find...

(a) 0.5 of 12 ⑥ $\qquad$ (b) 0.5 of 17 ⑧·⑤ $\qquad$ (c) 0.5 of 23 ⑪·⑤

(d) 0.25 of 16 ④ $\qquad$ (e) 0.25 of 40 ⑩ $\qquad$ (f) 0.25 of 72 ⑱

(g) 0.75 of 20 ⑮ $\qquad$ (h) 0.75 of 36 ㉗ $\qquad$ (i) 0.75 of 56 ㊷

2 Write as decimals:

(a) $\frac{3}{100}$ $\quad$ (b) $2\frac{7}{100}$ $\quad$ (c) $\frac{25}{100}$ $\quad$ (d) $3\frac{1}{4}$ $\quad$ (e) $4\frac{91}{100}$ $\quad$ (f) $7\frac{3}{4}$

(0·03) $\quad$ (2·07) $\quad$ (0·25) $\quad$ (3·25) $\quad$ (4·91) $\quad$ (7·75)

3 Write as fractions:

(a) 0.9 $\quad$ (b) 0.04 $\quad$ (c) 1.07 $\quad$ (d) 3.94 $\quad$ (e) 3.75 $\quad$ (f) 7.5

($\frac{9}{10}$) $\quad$ ($\frac{4}{100}$) $\quad$ ($1\frac{7}{100}$) $\quad$ ($3\frac{94}{100}$) $\quad$ ($3\frac{3}{4}$) $\quad$ ($7\frac{1}{2}$)

4

(a) There were 100 peaches in a box. 17 of them rotted. What decimal fraction of the peaches went rotten?

(0·17)

(b) 100 trees grew in a wood. 23 of them were cut down. What decimal fraction of the trees were cut down?

(0·23)

(c) We hired 100 cups for a party. 31 of them were broken. What decimal fraction of the cups were broken?

(0·31)

5 What decimal fraction should go at **a**? (0·5)

6 What decimal fraction should go at **b**? (1·2)

Multiplication and division

Multiplying and dividing

$$
\begin{array}{r} 3.6 \\ \times\ 4 \\ \hline 14.4 \end{array}
\qquad
\begin{array}{r} 2.57 \\ \times\ 3 \\ \hline 7.71 \end{array}
\qquad
\begin{array}{r} 3.94 \\ \times 10 \\ \hline 39.40 \end{array}
\qquad
5)\overline{18.5}\ \ 3.7
\qquad
6)\overline{8.76}\ \ 1.46
$$

1 Multiply

(a) $\begin{array}{r} 1.8 \\ \times\ 6 \\ \hline 10\cdot8 \end{array}$
  (b) $\begin{array}{r} 2.9 \\ \times\ 7 \\ \hline 20\cdot3 \end{array}$
  (c) $\begin{array}{r} 7.6 \\ \times\ 7 \\ \hline 53\cdot2 \end{array}$
  (d) $\begin{array}{r} 9.3 \\ \times\ 9 \\ \hline 83\cdot7 \end{array}$

(e) $\begin{array}{r} 2.34 \\ \times\ 4 \\ \hline 9\cdot36 \end{array}$
  (f) $\begin{array}{r} 3.96 \\ \times\ 3 \\ \hline 11\cdot88 \end{array}$
  (g) $\begin{array}{r} 5.76 \\ \times\ 8 \\ \hline 46\cdot08 \end{array}$
  (h) $\begin{array}{r} 3.46 \\ \times\ 7 \\ \hline 24\cdot22 \end{array}$
  (i) $\begin{array}{r} 5.69 \\ \times\ 8 \\ \hline 45\cdot52 \end{array}$

(j) $\begin{array}{r} 4.3 \\ \times 10 \\ \hline 43 \end{array}$
  (k) $\begin{array}{r} 7.6 \\ \times 10 \\ \hline 76 \end{array}$
  (l) $\begin{array}{r} 9.4 \\ \times 10 \\ \hline 94 \end{array}$
  (m) $\begin{array}{r} 8.3 \\ \times 10 \\ \hline 83 \end{array}$
  (n) $\begin{array}{r} 7.8 \\ \times 10 \\ \hline 78 \end{array}$

(o) $\begin{array}{r} 1.26 \\ \times 10 \\ \hline 12\cdot6 \end{array}$
  (p) $\begin{array}{r} 3.89 \\ \times 10 \\ \hline 38\cdot9 \end{array}$
  (q) $\begin{array}{r} 4.68 \\ \times 10 \\ \hline 46\cdot8 \end{array}$
  (r) $\begin{array}{r} 9.38 \\ \times 10 \\ \hline 93\cdot8 \end{array}$
  (s) $\begin{array}{r} 7.68 \\ \times 10 \\ \hline 76\cdot8 \end{array}$

2 Divide

(a) $2)\overline{9.6}\ \ 4\cdot8$
  (b) $3)\overline{10.8}\ \ 3\cdot6$
  (c) $4)\overline{15.6}\ \ 3\cdot9$

(d) $5)\overline{24.35}\ \ 4\cdot87$
  (e) $2)\overline{19.76}\ \ 9\cdot88$
  (f) $3)\overline{17.04}\ \ 5\cdot68$
  (g) $4)\overline{30.16}\ \ 7\cdot54$

(h) $5)\overline{39.80}\ \ 7\cdot96$
  (i) $9)\overline{20.52}\ \ 2\cdot28$
  (j) $8)\overline{13.12}\ \ 1\cdot64$
  (k) $6)\overline{40.56}\ \ 6\cdot76$
  (l) $7)\overline{30.52}\ \ 4\cdot36$

Revision

Write the answers.

1
(a) 9 +8 = 17
(b) 7 +6 = 13
(c) 7 +9 = 16
(d) 7 +19 = 26
(e) 11 −6 = 5
(f) 12 −4 = 8
(g) 15 −7 = 8
(h) 16 −9 = 7
(i) 17 −8 = 9

2
(a) 7 6 +5 = 18
(b) 8 7 +4 = 19
(c) 9 8 +6 = 23
(d) 8 8 +9 = 25
(e) 9 6 +7 = 22
(f) 9 8 +5 = 22
(g) 9 9 +3 = 21
(h) 8 7 +5 = 20
(i) 9 7 +8 = 24

3
(a) 4 ×6 = 24
(b) 9 ×3 = 27
(c) 8 ×7 = 56
(d) 6 ×9 = 54
(e) 4 ×0 = 0
(f) 6 ×5 = 30
(g) 9 ×2 = 18
(h) 9 ×4 = 36
(i) 9 ×8 = 72

4
(a) 2)14 = 7
(b) 3)27 = 9
(c) 6)42 = 7
(d) 4)56 = 14
(e) 5)25 = 5
(f) 7)63 = 9

5
(a) $(5 \times 7) + 6 = 41$
(b) $(3 \times 9) + 5 = 32$
(c) $(4 \times 7) + 6 = 34$
(d) $(5 \times 9) + 7 = 52$
(e) $(8 \times 9) + 6 = 78$
(f) $(6 \times 8) + 9 = 57$

'Hope you do well'

6
(a) $41 \div 6 = 6\ r5$
(b) $32 \div 5 = 6\ r2$
(c) $51 \div 6 = 8\ r3$
(d) $19 \div 4 = 4\ r3$
(e) $23 \div 8 = 2\ r7$
(f) $59 \div 9 = 6\ r5$

7 Round to the nearest 1000:

(a) 3187 (3000)
(b) 5666 (6000)
(c) 8500 (9000)
(d) 19 701 (20 000)
(e) 2876 (3000)
(f) 12 499 (12 000)

8 Estimate and round to the nearest 1000:

(a) 3904 + 1299 5000
(b) 9150 − 2080 7000
(c) 193 × 7 1000
(d) 307 × 29 9000
(e) $\frac{3}{4}$ of 780 1000
(f) 478 ÷ 5 0
(g) 2908 ÷ 5 0
(h) 11 047 − 3899 7000
(i) 3104 × 19 59 000

Revision

1 Write in numbers two hundred thousand and fifty. (200050)

2 How many minutes from 2.25pm until 3.15pm? (50)

3 $30 - (\frac{1}{5} \text{ of } 35) = \boxed{23}$

4 0.1 of 30 = $\boxed{3}$

5 Write $\frac{1}{4}$ as a decimal. $(0 \cdot 25)$

6 $1000 - 299 = \boxed{701}$

7 Sam baked 42 buns. He put them on 6 plates. How many were on each plate? (7)

8 Write 0.9 as a fraction. $(\frac{9}{10})$

9 $\frac{7}{100} = 0.\boxed{07}$

10 $18 + 49 + 7 = \boxed{74}$

11 $6 - 0.8 = \boxed{5 \cdot 2}$

12 $34 \times 2 \times 1 = \boxed{68}$

13 Write $\frac{37}{100}$ as a decimal. $(0 \cdot 37)$

14 $6 \times 400 = \boxed{2400}$

15 $6 \overline{)51}$
    $\underline{8} \, r3$

16 $2\frac{1}{5} = \boxed{22}$ tenths.

17 $17 \times 16 \times 0 = \boxed{0}$

18 $0.4 + 0.7 + 1.0 = \boxed{2 \cdot 1}$

19 There are 20 cars in a park. $\frac{1}{4}$ are red, $\frac{1}{5}$ are blue, and the rest green. How many are green? (11)

20 $3\frac{23}{100} = 3 + \frac{\boxed{2}}{10} + \frac{\boxed{3}}{100}$

Revision

1

(a) 49 + 4876 + 8 + 15 399 = $\boxed{20332}$ (b) 10 000 − 1043 = $\boxed{8957}$

(c) 596 + 59 + 17 488 + 7 = $\boxed{18150}$ (d) 20 000 − 6204 = $\boxed{13796}$

2 Change the numbers in the brackets to decimals and add them together.

(a) (2 units + 9 tenths + 7 hundredths) $\boxed{2\cdot97}$

(b) (6 units + 7 tenths) $\boxed{6\cdot7}$ (c) $(3 + \frac{9}{10})$ $\boxed{3\cdot9}$

3 This truck can hold 56 cases of lemonade.
Each case holds 36 bottles.
How many bottles are on the truck? (2016)

4 Write the following as decimals:

(a) $\frac{3}{10}$ (b) $\frac{1}{2}$ (c) $\frac{1}{5}$ (d) $\frac{4}{5}$ (e) $\frac{9}{100}$ (f) $\frac{37}{100}$ (g) $\frac{207}{100}$

0·3   0·5   0·2   0·8   0·09   0·37   2·07

5 Write these in order, smallest first:

(a) 1.2, 1, 1.02, 1.22.   1, 1·02, 1·2, 1·22

(b) 3, 0.03, 3.03, 3.33.   0·03, 3, 3·03, 3·33

(c) 0.5, 5.5, 5.05, 0.05.   0·05, 0·5, 5·05, 5·5

6 Write the missing numbers:

(a) $0.37 = \frac{3}{10} + \frac{\boxed{7}}{100}$ (d) $1.26 = 1 + \frac{\boxed{2}}{10} + \frac{\boxed{6}}{100}$

(b) $0.52 = \frac{5}{\boxed{10}} + \frac{2}{100}$ (e) $2.07 = 2 + \frac{\boxed{0}}{10} + \frac{\boxed{7}}{100}$

(c) $0.63 = \frac{6}{\boxed{10}} + \frac{\boxed{3}}{100}$ (f) $4.20 = 4 + \frac{\boxed{2}}{10} + \frac{\boxed{0}}{100}$

Decimals - Addition and subtraction

Adding and subtracting.

1.34 2.08 + 2.95 —— 6.37	$\begin{array}{r} 7.12 \\ -3.48 \\ \hline \end{array}$ → $\begin{array}{r} 7.^0\cancel{1}2 \\ -3.48 \\ \hline 4 \end{array}$ → $\begin{array}{r} ^6 7.^{10}\cancel{1}2 \\ -3.48 \\ \hline 3.64 \end{array}$

We must keep the decimal points under each other.

1 Write the answers.

(a) $\begin{array}{r} 2.16 \\ + 5.99 \\ \hline 8 \cdot 15 \end{array}$

(b) $\begin{array}{r} 7.85 \\ + 2.96 \\ \hline 10 \cdot 81 \end{array}$

(c) $\begin{array}{r} 4.09 \\ + 3.78 \\ \hline 7 \cdot 87 \end{array}$

(d) $\begin{array}{r} 12.48 \\ + 8.94 \\ \hline 21 \cdot 42 \end{array}$

(e) $\begin{array}{r} 1.34 \\ 1.98 \\ + 2.79 \\ \hline 6 \cdot 11 \end{array}$

(f) $\begin{array}{r} 6.84 \\ 3.96 \\ + 2.87 \\ \hline 13 \cdot 67 \end{array}$

(g) $\begin{array}{r} 5.66 \\ 4.93 \\ + 1.08 \\ \hline 11 \cdot 67 \end{array}$

(h) $\begin{array}{r} 7.39 \\ 13.46 \\ + 12.88 \\ \hline 33 \cdot 73 \end{array}$

(i) $\begin{array}{r} 9.86 \\ - 1.45 \\ \hline 8 \cdot 41 \end{array}$

(j) $\begin{array}{r} 7.67 \\ - 2.15 \\ \hline 5 \cdot 52 \end{array}$

(k) $\begin{array}{r} 8.83 \\ - 2.70 \\ \hline 6 \cdot 13 \end{array}$

(l) $\begin{array}{r} 6.21 \\ - 1.47 \\ \hline 4 \cdot 74 \end{array}$

(m) $\begin{array}{r} 8.13 \\ - 2.49 \\ \hline 5 \cdot 64 \end{array}$

(n) $\begin{array}{r} 9.23 \\ - 1.58 \\ \hline 7 \cdot 65 \end{array}$

(o) $\begin{array}{r} 10.01 \\ - 4.17 \\ \hline 5 \cdot 84 \end{array}$

(p) $\begin{array}{r} 10.01 \\ - 3.49 \\ \hline 6 \cdot 52 \end{array}$

2 By how much is 9.03 greater than 1.46? (7·57)

3 What must be added to each of these numbers to make it equal to 10:

(a) 3.14 (6·86) (b) 2.09 (7·91) (c) 7.35 (2·65) (d) 5.04 (4·96) (e) 6.26 (3·74) (f) 8.46 (1·54)

4 By how much is 3.46 smaller than 7.01? (3·55)

Length

12 centimetres (cm)

This cm is divided into 10 millimetres (mm).

---

1 Estimate the length of each line in cm.

2 Measure each line, in cm.

3 Measure each line in mm.

(a) ▬▬▬▬▬ 3cm , 30mm

(b) ▬▬▬▬▬▬▬ 5cm , 50mm

(c) ▬▬▬▬▬▬▬▬▬ 8·5cm , 85mm

(d) ▬▬▬▬▬▬▬▬▬▬ 10cm , 100mm

4 Draw lines that you think are (a) 2cm, (b) 9cm, (c) 45mm, (d) 65mm.

5 Measure each line. What was your error?

---

6 Write each of the following in a similar way.

16mm = 1cm 6mm or 1.6cm.

(a) 18mm = 1cm 8mm or 1·8cm

(b) 54mm = 5cm 4mm or 5·4cm

(c) 27mm = 2cm 7mm or 2·7cm

(d) 65mm = 6cm 5mm or 6·5cm

(e) 32mm = 3cm 2mm or 3·2cm

(f) 20mm = 2cm 0mm or 2cm

(g) 14mm = 1cm 4mm or 1·4cm

(h) 77mm = 7cm 7mm or 7·7cm

7

(a)
cm	mm
2	3
1	4
+ 3	2
6	9

(b)
cm	mm
2	6
1	4
+ 1	5
5	5

(c)
cm	mm
3	7
1	5
+ 1	6
6	8

(d)
cm	mm
4	9
1	7
+ 2	8
9	4

(e)
cm	mm
5	8
2	9
+ 1	6
10	3

(f)
cm	mm
6	9
− 1	4
5	5

(g)
cm	mm
7	1
− 2	4
4	7

(h)
cm	mm
9	3
− 1	7
7	6

(i)
cm	mm
9	3
− 4	7
4	6

(j)
cm	mm
8	2
− 4	7
3	5

Length

100 centimetres = 1 metre

1cm = $\frac{1}{100}$ metre or 0.01 metre.

1

Write each of the following in m and cm.

146cm = 1m 46cm	= $1\frac{46}{100}$ m	= 1.46m
209cm = 2m 9cm	= $2\frac{9}{100}$ m	= 2.09m

(a) 134cm = | 1m 34 cm |

(b) 194cm = | 1m 94 cm |

(c) 69cm = | 0m 69cm |

(d) 203cm = | 2m 3cm |

(e) 329cm = | 3m 29cm |

(f) 361cm = | 3m 61cm |

---

2 How many cm in each of these?

(a) 1m 3cm (103) **(b)** 2m 37cm (237) **(c)** 0.67m (67) **(d)** 1.74m (174)

(e) 1.05m (105) **(f)** 1m 52cm (152) **(g)** 2.83m (283) **(h)** 0.08m (8)

3

(a)

m	cm
1	13
2	27
+ 2	34
5	74

(b)

m	cm
1	56
3	47
+ 3	59
8	62

(c)

m	cm
2	56
4	68
+ 3	78
11	02

(d)

m	cm
4	96
3	97
+ 1	85
10	78

(e)

m	cm
4	09
2	76
+ 3	93
10	78

(f)

m	cm
7	18
2	97
+ 3	85
14	00

(g)

m	cm
3	07
3	76
+ 2	89
9	72

(h)

m	cm
2	95
4	86
+ 5	79
13	60

(i)

m	cm
6	10
− 1	30
4	80

(j)

m	cm
7	20
− 3	90
3	30

(k)

m	cm
8	12
− 2	24
5	88

(l)

m	cm
6	8
− 1	39
4	69

(m)

m	cm
9	15
− 1	79
7	36

(n)

m	cm
10	04
− 2	09
7	95

(o)

m	cm
11	14
− 3	76
7	38

(p)

m	cm
12	37
− 4	49
7	88

Length

1 A rope is 4.45m long. Two pieces, one measuring 75cm and the other measuring $2\frac{1}{2}$ m, are cut off. What length is left? $\boxed{1\cdot2m}$

2

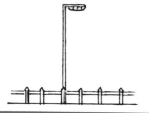

The height of the lamp post is 4.8m.
The height of the fence is 0.83m.

Find the difference in their height. $\boxed{3\cdot97m}$

3 A pencil is 17cm long. Another pencil is 2.4cm shorter. If they are put end to end what is the total length? $\boxed{31\cdot6cm}$

4
A rope is 10m long. Three pieces measuring 2.5m, 1.25m and 1.45m are cut off.

What length of rope is left? $\boxed{4\cdot8m}$

5

(a)  2.27m

3.24m

The total length of the 3 sides of this triangle measures 6.69m.
What is the length of side **(a)**? $\boxed{1\cdot18m}$

6

(a) m	(b) m	(c) m	(d) m	(e) m	(f) m
2.47	2.86	5.63	8.07	7.68	4.58
x 3	x 4	x 6	x 4	x 7	x 6
7·41	11·44	33·78	32·28	53·76	27·48

7 One box is 1.14m high.

What is the total height of a stack of 9 boxes? $\boxed{10\cdot26m}$

8 One paving stone is 0.84m long. It takes 9 stones to make a path.

What is the length of the path? $\boxed{7\cdot56m}$

Length

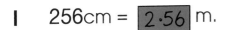

1   256cm = `2·56` m.

2   400cm = `4` m.

3   How many cm less than 3m is $2\frac{3}{4}$ m?   *25 cm.*

4   6.04m = `604` cm.

5   2cm – 1mm = `1·99` cm.

6   $3\frac{1}{2}$ cm = `350` mm.

7   3m – 65cm = `2·35` m.

8   444cm = `4·44` m.

9   $2\frac{1}{10}$ m = `210` cm.

10   A piece of cord 35cm long is cut from a piece 2m long. What length is left? *(1·65 m.)*

11   1m 45cm + 1m 55cm = `3m`

12   4m – 1.2m = `2·8m`

13   By how much is 3m longer than 2m 9cm?   *91 cm.*

14   508cm = `5·08` m.

15   4.18m = `418` cm.

16   2cm – 7mm = `1·93` cm.

17   $4\frac{9}{10}$ m = `490` cm.

18   Finish these sequences:

(a)   0.64cm, 0.66cm, 0.68cm, `0·70cm` , `0·72cm` , `0·74cm` .

(b)   0.05cm, 0.1cm,   0.15cm, `0·2 cm` , `0·25cm` , `0·3 cm` .

(c)   0.92cm, 0.95cm, 0.98cm, `1·01cm` , `1·04cm` , `1·07cm` .

(d)   2.04cm, 2.06cm, 2.08cm, `2·1cm` , `2·12cm` , `2·14cm` .

(e)   3.11cm, 3.14cm, 3.17cm, `3·2 cm` , `3·23cm` , `3·26cm` .

(f)   5.25cm, 5.29cm, 5.33cm, `5·37cm` , `5·41cm` , `5·45cm` .

Length – Kilometres

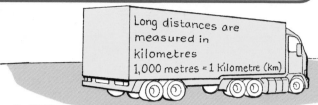

Long distances are measured in kilometres
1,000 metres = 1 Kilometre (km)

2476m = 2km 476m   2009m = 2km 9m

1 Write the following in a similar way.

(a) 1056m = 1km 56m   (b) 1250m = 1km 250m   (c) 1008m = 1km 8m

(d) 2094m = 2km 94m   (e) 2790m = 2km 790m   (f) 2407m = 2km 407m

(g) 4007m = 4km 7m   (h) 5200m = 5km 200m   (i) 5064m = 5km 64m

2

(a)
km	m
1	246
1	189
+ 2	76
4	511

(b)
km	m
2	587
2	798
+ 3	719
9	104

(c)
km	m
4	87
3	798
+ 3	407
11	292

(d)
km	m
5	96
1	787
+ 2	956
9	839

(e)
km	m
7	100
− 2	600
4	500

(f)
km	m
8	200
− 3	700
4	500

(g)
km	m
9	400
− 4	900
4	500

(h)
km	m
10	200
− 1	400
8	800

3 A truck driver had 410km to travel. He drove 80km 400m in the morning and $124\frac{1}{2}$km in the afternoon.

How far had he still to travel? (205km 100m)

4 Susan drove $104\frac{1}{2}$ km on Friday, $98\frac{1}{4}$km on Saturday and $134\frac{3}{4}$ km on Sunday. How far did she drive that weekend?  (337km 500m) or (337½ km)

5 Frank set out to cycle 210km. He cycled 47km on the first day. How far had he still to cycle? (163km)

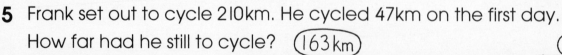

6

(e)
km	m
10	400
− 2	650
7	750

(b)
km	m
9	200
− 1	430
7	770

(c)
km	m
12	340
− 4	450
7	890

(d)
km	m
13	130
− 1	270
11	860

Revision – Weight

Remember $\Bigg\} \rightarrow$

1 kilogramme	=	1000g
$\frac{1}{2}$ kg	=	500g
0.1 kg	=	100g
0.25kg	=	250g

A gramme is a very light weight.

1 0.5kg = $\boxed{500}$ grammes.

2 1.5kg = $\boxed{1500}$ grammes.

3 $2\frac{1}{4}$kg = $\boxed{2250}$ grammes.

4 2.1kg = $\boxed{2100}$ grammes.

5 $3\frac{3}{4}$kg = $\boxed{3750}$ grammes.

6 3.6kg = $\boxed{3600}$ grammes.

7 2400g = $\boxed{2}$ kg $\boxed{400}$ g.

8 4760g = $\boxed{4}$ kg $\boxed{760}$ g.

9 The weight of one parcel is 350g and that of another is 650g. Find the total weight.
$\boxed{\text{1 kilogramme}}$

10 1kg – 450g = $\boxed{550\,g}$

11 1.5kg – 900g = $\boxed{600\,g}$

12 1750g + $\frac{1}{4}$ kg = $\boxed{2}$ kg.

13 3kg – 250g = $\boxed{2\,kg\,750\,g}$

14 1kg – 640g = $\boxed{360\,g}$

15 2kg – 900g = $\boxed{1\,kg\,100\,g}$

16 4.9kg = $\boxed{4900}$ g.

17 How many grammes must be added to 800g to make 1.5kg? $\boxed{700\,g}$

18 Put the following in order, lightest first:

495g $\frac{1}{2}$kg   1.75kg   1400g

495g , $\frac{1}{2}$kg , 1400g , 1·75kg

19 4405g = $\boxed{4}$ kg $\boxed{405}$ g.

20 4901g = $\boxed{4}$ kg $\boxed{901}$ g.

21 2kg – 950g = $\boxed{1\,kg\,50\,g}$

Revision – Weight

	kg	g			kg	g			kg	g			kg	g
1	2	450		**2**	4	190		**3**	5	290		**4**	6	550
	+ 3	170			+ 3	480			+ 2	799			+ 3	689
	5	620			7	670			8	089			10	239

	kg	g			kg	g			kg	g			kg	g
5	1	396		**6**	3	609		**7**	2	685		**8**	4	482
	2	487			2	854			4	984			3	867
	+ 3	509			+ 7	789			+ 3	789			+ 3	706
	7	392			14	252			11	458			12	055

	kg	g			kg	g			kg	g			kg	g
9	4	700		**10**	7	900		**11**	9	500		**12**	8	600
	− 1	450			− 2	610			− 1	104			− 3	420
	3	250			5	290			8	396			5	180

	kg	g			kg	g			kg	g			kg	g
13	7	100		**14**	8	200		**15**	6	400		**16**	9	300
	− 3	400			− 1	900			− 1	500			− 2	400
	3	700			6	300			4	900			6	900

17

 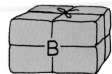

Parcel **A** has a weight of 2kg 750g.
Parcel **B** is 380g heavier than parcel **A**.
Find the total weight
of the 2 parcels. 5kg 880g

18

A sack of sugar had a weight of 7kg. 2kg 340g
were used. What weight of sugar was left?
4kg 660g

19

A piece of meat had a weight of 7kg 150g.
What weight of meat was left when two pieces
weighing 3kg 320g and 1kg 75g were cut off?
2kg 755g

Revision – Weight

kg g	kg g
3 450 ×5 ————— 17 250	5) 7 150 1 430

1 kg g
   3 450
     ×5
 17 250

2 kg g
   4 360
     ×6
 26 160

3 kg g
   2 850
     ×4
 11 400

4 kg g
   3 570
     ×8
 28 560

5 kg g
 5) 7 150
   1 430

6 kg g
 6) 9 240
   1 540

7 kg g
 4) 9 520
   2 380

8 kg g
 8) 10 160
   1 270

9 A family used 1kg 230g of sugar per week.

What mass of sugar was used in 7 weeks?

`8kg 610g`

10

How many cubes in this pile? (Be careful!)

`10`

If the total weight of the cubes is
10kg 215g find the weight of one cube.

`1kg 135g`

11 Tom weighs 24kg 240g.
Dad is three times as heavy as Tom.
Find the combined weight of Tom and Dad.

`96kg 960g`

12 The total weight of twin babies was 6kg 110g.
The baby girl was 150g lighter than the baby boy.
Find the weight of each.

`Boy : 3kg 130g`
`Girl : 2kg 980g`

Number facts

Number facts are very important.
Always have them at your fingertips.

1
(a)	(b)	(c)	(d)	(e)	(f)	(g)	(h)
4	8	3	6	6	7	8	6
9	5	4	5	9	8	6	8
3	7	8	9	8	9	9	9
+ 7	+ 6	+ 9	+ 7	+ 5	+ 4	+ 5	+ 4
23	26	24	27	28	28	28	27

2
(a)	(b)	(c)	(d)	(e)	(f)	(g)	(h)
14	13	15	12	9	16	17	15
− 6	− 9	− 7	− 4	− 0	− 9	− 8	− 9
8	4	8	8	9	7	9	6

3
(a)	(b)	(c)	(d)	(e)	(f)	(g)	(h)
4	9	8	7	6	5	4	6
x 7	x 3	x 5	x 7	x 9	x 7	x 9	x 8
28	27	40	49	54	35	36	48

4 (a) $63 \div 7$ (b) $48 \div 6$ (c) $28 \div 4$ (d) $48 \div 8$ (e) $54 \div 9$

5 (a) $3 \overline{)10}$ (b) $4 \overline{)17}$ (c) $5 \overline{)29}$ (d) $6 \overline{)38}$ (e) $7 \overline{)40}$

  (a) 3r1 (b) 4r1 (c) 5r4 (d) 6r2 (e) 5r5

6 Fractions and decimals quiz!

(a) Write 0.9 as a fraction. $\frac{9}{10}$

(b) Write 0.07 as a fraction. $\frac{7}{100}$

(c) Write $\frac{7}{10}$ as a decimal. $0 \cdot 7$

(d) Write $\frac{6}{100}$ as a decimal. $0 \cdot 06$

(e) Write $\frac{3}{5}$ as a decimal. $0 \cdot 6$

(f) 0.1 of 90 = 9

(g) 0.01 of 200= 2

(h) 0.01 of 6 = $0 \cdot 06$

(i) $\frac{4}{9}$ of 36 = 16

(j) $3 - 0.7 =$ $2 \cdot 3$

(k) $0.49 = \frac{4}{10} + \frac{9}{100}$

(l) $\frac{5}{8}$ of 32 = 20

(m) $\frac{1}{2} = \frac{4}{8}$

(n) Write $\frac{3}{4}$ as a decimal. $0 \cdot 75$

(o) Write $\frac{15}{4}$ as a decimal. $3 \cdot 75$

(p) $\frac{3}{100} + \frac{7}{100} = 0 . \boxed{1}$

(q) $2 - 0.1 =$ $1 \cdot 9$

(r) $0.6 + 0.19 =$ $0 \cdot 79$

Revision

1   What number is **4** times greater than **30**? (120)

2   How many tenths in **6.5**? (65)

3   **30**cm + [20] cm = $\frac{1}{2}$ m.

4   $\frac{1}{4}$ = $\frac{[2]}{8}$.

5   **4** x **196** x **0** = [0]

6   **1**hr **50**mins = [110] mins.

7   Name **4** factors of:
(a)**12**   1, 2, 3, 4, 6, 12
(b)**30**   1, 2, 3, 5, 6, 10, 15, 30

8   What number is **3** greater than **9998**? (10001)

9   $\frac{1}{2}$ kg − **200**g = [300g]

10   **25** + **100** + **25** + **21** = [171]

11   $\frac{2}{5}$ = $\frac{[4]}{10}$

12   A train should have left at **2.55**pm, but was **20** mins late leaving. At what time did it leave? (3·15 pm)

13   A packet weighs **250**g. How many packets weigh **2**$\frac{1}{4}$ kg? (9)

14   **200** ÷ **25** = [8]

15   Write in figures: one million and sixty thousand. (1060000)

16   Is a person's weight measured in kilometres or kilogrammes? (kilogrammes)

17   $9\overline{)72}$
        $\underline{8}$

18   Find the number that is $\frac{1}{2}$ way between **64** and **70**. (67)

19   Round to the nearest **1000**:
(a) 4099   (4000)
(b) 6500   (7000)
(c) 9821   (10000)

Revision

1   Multiply each number by 39.

(a)   24   **(b)**   106   **(c)**   287   **(d)**   2568   **(e)**   1006
     936   4134   11193   100152   39234

2   Insert the missing signs (+, −, x, or ÷).

(a) $20 \boxed{-} 8 = 4 \boxed{\times} 3$ **(b)** $28 \boxed{+} 12 = 8 \boxed{\times} 5$

(c) $10 \boxed{-} 3 = 21 \boxed{\div} 3$ **(d)** $48 \boxed{\div} 6 = 2 \boxed{\times} 4$

(e) $100 \boxed{\div} 10 = 5 \boxed{\times} 2$ 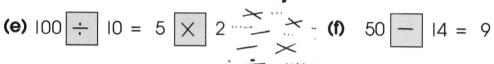 **(f)** $50 \boxed{-} 14 = 9 \boxed{\times} 4$

3

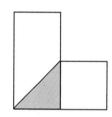

(a)   What fraction of this shape is shaded? $\left(\dfrac{1}{6}\right)$

(b)   If the whole shape is worth 354 points find the value of the white part. $\left(295 \text{ points}\right)$

4   **(a)** $19\overline{)961}$ 50 r 11   **(b)** $29\overline{)857}$ 29 r 16   **(c)** $17\overline{)625}$ 36 r 13   **(d)** $53\overline{)1471}$ 27 r 40   **(e)** $37\overline{)1073}$ 29

5   Find the missing numbers.

(a) $841 = 800 + \boxed{40} + 1$

(b) $2937 = \boxed{2000} + 900 + 30 + 7$

(c) $6804 = 6000 + \boxed{800} + 0 + 4$

(d) $15\ 407 = 10\ 000 + \boxed{5000} + 400 + 0 + 7$

(e) $24\ 629 = \boxed{20\ 000} + 4000 + 600 + 20 + 9$

Revision

1 True or false?

	true	false
(a) $9 \times 8 > 11 \times 7$		✓
(b) $(8 \div 4) \div 2 = 8 \div (4 \div 2)$.		✓
(c) $1.9 < 1\frac{9}{10}$.		✓
(d) $2.5\,cm + 0.6\,cm = 3.1\,cm$.	✓	
(e) $3kg\ 44g + 2kg\ 90g = 1634g$		✓

2

(a) $3.1 + 7 + 4.89 + 0.$ $\boxed{14\cdot99}$

(b) $6.01 - 0.8$ $\boxed{5\cdot21}$

(c) $4.37 + 0.9 + 3 + 1.7$ $\boxed{9\cdot97}$

(d) $10 - 2.04$ $\boxed{7\cdot96}$

(e) $08.98 + 7 + 9.88 + 3.9$ $\boxed{29\cdot76}$

(f) $11.2 - 3.43$ $\boxed{7\cdot77}$

3

8 buses were used to take 347 people to a pop concert. 7 of the buses were full with 46 in each.

How many were on the other bus? $\boxed{25}$

4

A game of soccer started at 3.15pm. Each half lasted 35mins and there was a half-time interval of 10mins.
At what time did the game end? $\boxed{4 \cdot 35\,pm}$

5

A plank of timber was 12m long. Two pieces measuring 2m 9cm and 6m 48cm were cut off.
What length of timber was left?

$\boxed{3m\ 43cm}$

Capacity

I litre = 1000 millilitres (mls)

A teaspoon holds about 5ml.

100ml

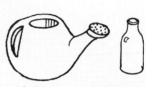

6 litres

1 litre

Quick answers here:

1 $\frac{1}{2}$ litre = 500 ml.

2 $1\frac{1}{2}$ litres = 1500 ml.

3 $1\frac{1}{4}$ litres = 1250 ml.

4 How many 250ml mugs can be filled from 1 litre? 4

5 2500ml = $2\frac{1}{2}$ l.

6 3250ml = $3\frac{1}{4}$ l.

7 How many 250ml mugs can be filled from $1\frac{3}{4}$ litres? 7

8 $1\frac{1}{4}$ litres = 1250ml = 1·25 l.

9 A bottle holds 300ml. How many bottles can be filled from $1\frac{1}{2}$ litres? 5

10 $2\frac{3}{4}$ litres = 2750 ml.

11 A barrel holds 100 litres. 80 half litres are poured from it. How many litres are left? 60

12 2.5 litres + 4000ml = 6·5 l.

13
l	ml
2	396
1	487
+ 2	509
6	392

14
l	ml
3	450
2	878
+ 7	740
14	068

15
l	ml
4	920
3	870
+ 3	789
12	579

16
l	ml
2	682
3	780
+ 1	985
8	447

17
l	ml
7	200
− 2	800
4	400

18
l	ml
9	100
− 2	700
6	400

19
l	ml
6	220
− 1	840
4	380

20
l	ml
8	430
− 2	750
5	680

21  A family uses $1\frac{1}{2}$ litres of milk a day. How many litres would they use in the month of April? 45 litres

Large numbers

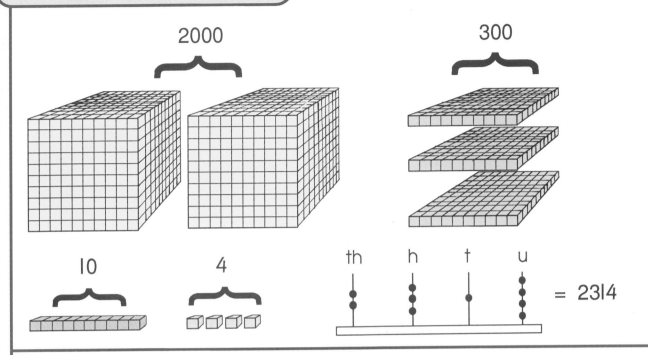

2000   300

10   4   th   h   t   u   = 2314

Write the correct numerals.

1   `2 2 6 7`

2   `2 2 0 5`

3   `3 0 7 6`

---

4   Add 100 to each number.

(a) 41   (b) 108   (c) 200   (d) 1015   (e) 2000   (f) 2008   (g) 3109
    141   208   300   1115   2100   2108   3209

---

5   Add 1000 to each number.

(a) 69   (b) 104   (c) 178   (d) 300   (e) 1049   (f) 2080   (g) 3005
    1069   1104   1178   1300   2049   3080   4005

Large numbers

1   Put the following in order; start with the least:

    a 59, 406, 8, 604, 1000.   8, 59, 406, 604, 1000

    b 220, 202, 20, 2, 200.   2, 20, 200, 202, 220

    c 3140, 1340, 4014, 1043, 3041. 1043, 1340, 3041, 3140, 4014

    d 1240, 2014, 1402, 1204, 2041. 1204, 1240, 1402, 2014, 2041

2   Add one to each number.

    (a) 999   **(b)** 1099   **(c)** 3000   **(d)** 2399   **(e)** 4990

       (1000)   (1100)   (3001)   (2400)   (4991)

3   Write the number shown on each abacus.

    (a) 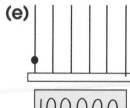   **(b)** 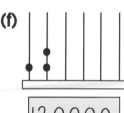   **(c)** 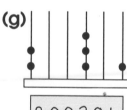   **(d)**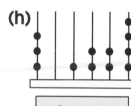

    101 000   200 300   310 410   204 030

    (e)   **(f)**   **(g)**   **(h)**

    100 000   120 000   200 301   301 224

4   Write a numeral for:

    (a) Ten thousand and four (10 004)

    (b) Twenty thousand and thirty six (20 036)

    (c) Fifty thousand one hundred and six (50 106)

    (d) One hundred thousand and twenty (100 020)

    (e) Two hundred and ten thousand five hundred (210 500)

    (f) Six hundred and ten thousand four hundred (610 400)

Large numbers

A **million** is a very large number.

| 1 000 000 (6 zeros) = one million. | 500 000 = $\frac{1}{2}$ million. |

1 Write the signs <, > or = for each.

(a) 1240 $\boxed{<}$ 1402

(b) 10 000 + 300 + 2 $\boxed{=}$ 10 302

(c) 5003 $\boxed{<}$ 5300

(d) 21 204 $\boxed{<}$ 21 402

2 Write the missing numbers.

(a) 4396 = $\boxed{4}$ thousands + $\boxed{3}$ hundreds + $\boxed{9}$ tens + $\boxed{6}$ units.

(b) 12 083 = $\boxed{12}$ thousands + $\boxed{0}$ hundreds + $\boxed{8}$ tens + $\boxed{3}$ units.

(c) 193 065 = $\boxed{193}$ thousands + $\boxed{0}$ hundreds + $\boxed{6}$ tens + $\boxed{5}$ units.

3 Write the following in words.

(a) 320 104 three hundred and twenty thousand one hundred and four

(b) 705 008 seven hundred and five thousand and eight

(c) 600 500 six hundred thousand five hundred

(d) 999 999 nine hundred and ninety nine thousand nine hundred and ninety nine

4 Write the next 2 numbers in each set.

(a) 39 997, 39 998, 39 999, 40 000, 40001

(b) 999 997, 999 998, 999 999, 1 000 000, 1 000 001

(c) 1 000 008, 1 000 009, 1000 010, 1000 011

5 Write the number that is one less than

(a) 12 000
11 999

(b) 50 000
49 999

(c) 100 000
99 999

(d) 32 000
31 999

6 Now write the following in a similar way.

| 30 000 + 1000 + 20 + 9 = 31 029 |

I'm big enough for these

(a) 50 000 + 9000 + 400 + 2 = $\boxed{59402}$

(b) 70 000 + 4000 + 7 = $\boxed{74007}$

Revision – Rounding off

10

We know we sometimes round numbers **up** or **down** to the nearest **10**.

We could say "There are about 50 peanuts in the bag", where there might be 53.

We know that a number ending in 5 is always rounded **up**, when rounding to the nearest **10**.

1   Round these to the nearest **10** (the first 3 are done for you).

(a) 17 → **20**   **(b)** 14 → **10**   **(c)** 98 → **100**

(d) 11 → 10   **(e)** 22 → 20   **(f)** 36 → 40

(g) 51 → 50   **(h)** 66 → 70   **(i)** 74 → 70

(j) 65 → 70   **(k)** 71 → 70   **(l)** 83 → 80

100

2   We can also round off to the nearest **100**.

256 becomes 300 because 256 is nearer 300 than to 200.

450 is half-way between 400 and 500. When this happens we round **up**.   450 → 500

Round these to the nearest **100**.

(a) 161 → 200   **(b)** 208 → 200   **(c)** 467 → 500

(d) 840 → 800   **(e)** 906 → 900   **(f)** 630 → 600

(g) 980 → 1000   **(h)** 916 → 900   **(i)** 370 → 400

1000

Rounding to the nearest **1000**.

1467:   The important digit here is 4. As 4 is less than 5 we will round **down**.   1476 → 1000.   1690 → 2000.   2500 → 3000.

3   Round these to the nearest 1000.

(a) 4090 → 4000   **(b)** 1596 → 2000   **(c)** 2222 → 2000

(d) 7209 → 7000   **(e)** 5555 → 6000   **(f)** 7500 → 8000

Estimation

Estimation is just a good guess.

A good guess is very useful!

Estimate the answer of 31 + 48.

31 is close to 30. (Round **down** to 30).
48 is close to 50. (Round **up** to 50).
30 + 50 = 80 (our estimate).

I Estimate the answer first, then work out the answer.

(a) 30 + 50 = 80 80

(b) 60 + 100 = 160 160

(c) 32 + 54 = 80 86

(d) 236 + 449 = 600 685

(e) 64 + 97 = 160 161

(f) 774 + 926 = 1700 1700

What is a good estimate of 43 x 6?

43 is very close to 40 (rounded **down**).
So 40 x 6 = 240.
So 240 is a good estimate of 43 x 6.

Right answer = 258

2 What is a good estimate of 256 x 7?
256 is very close to 260 (rounded **up**).

 1800

3 What is a good estimate of 54 x 37?   2000

4 Give a good estimate for these.

(a) 58 x 6 = 360

(b) 83 x 7 = 560

(c) 74 x 9 = 630

(d) 51 x 6 = 300

(e) 98 x 4 = 400

(f) 22 x 9 = 180

(g) 311 x 6 = 1800

(h) 608 x 4 = 2400

(i) 44 x 61 = 2400

(j) 96 x 45 = 5000

(k) 67 x 42 = 2800

(l) 84 x 37 = 3200

Revision

1	8 + 9 =	17
2	18 + 9 =	27
3	7 + 6 =	13
4	17 + 6 =	23
5	6 + 8 =	14
6	16 + 8 =	24
7	42 + 6 =	48
8	10 − 3 =	7
9	12 − 15 =	7
10	16 − 7 =	9
11	15 − 9 =	6
12	17 − 8 =	9
13	14 − 8 =	6
14	13 − 4 =	9
15	8 x 6 =	48
16	9 x 4 =	36

Hope I know these!

17	7 x 6 =	42
18	3 x 7 =	21
19	2 x 8 =	16
20	7 x 10 =	70
21	7 x 7 =	49
22	16 ÷ 2 =	8
23	14 ÷ 2 =	7
24	18 ÷ 3 =	6
25	21 ÷ 7 =	3
26	30 ÷ 5 =	6
27	35 ÷ 5 =	7
28	56 ÷ 8 =	7
29	36 : 4 =	9
30	27 ÷ 3 =	9
31	56 ÷ 7 =	8
32	48 ÷ 8 =	6

I never forget!

33	3 x 9 = 9 x 3
34	5 x 10 = 10 x 5
35	7 x 9 = 9 x 7
36	6 x 5 = 5 x 6
37	8 x 7 = 7 x 8

38	(8 x 10) + 6 =	86
39	(7 x 4) + 9 =	37
40	(8 x 6) + 7 =	55
41	50 − (7 x 7) =	1
42	70 − (7 x 9) =	7

43 In a school there are 7 classes.
One day 9 pupils were absent in each class.
How many pupils in all were absent that day?

63

Basic Rules of Number: Stage 6

© Folens

Addition and subtraction

Estimate first.

	1	2	3	4	5
	48	86	54	98	47
	36	59	89	27	69
	+ 25	+ 37	+ 76	+ 36	+ 34
	109	182	219	161	150

	6	7	8	9	10
	474	389	736	409	708
	398	107	398	37	309
	+ 57	+485	+577	+ 58	+104
	929	981	1711	504	1121

11 368 + 4 + 27 + 108 = 507

13 567 + 58 + 7 + 24 = 656

15 95 + 6 + 250 + 308 = 659

17 8 + 358 + 9 + 425 = 800

19 39 + 458 + 7 + 307 = 811

12 99 − 24 = 75

14 85 − 30 = 55

16 70 − 23 = 47

18 100 − 31 = 69

20 201 − 46 = 155

21 There are 310 children in a school. 193 are boys.

How many are girls? 117

22 A farmer has 250 sheep. He sells 104.

How many does he have left? 146

23 329 workers go to the factory by car, 84 walk and 158 go by bus.

How many workers go to the factory?  571

24	25	26	27	28
1892	77	29	38	13 987
498	1489	476	4193	4 395
27	36	3989	576	387
+ 4609	+ 599	+ 5	+ 8	+1 496
7026	2201	4499	4815	20265

Multiplication and division

1

(a) $12 \div 2 = \boxed{6}$ (b) $30 \div 5 = \boxed{6}$ (c) $16 \div 8 = \boxed{2}$

(d) $8 \div 4 = \boxed{2}$ (e) $25 \div 5 = \boxed{5}$ (f) $45 \div 5 = \boxed{9}$

(g) $20 \div 4 = \boxed{5}$ (h) $32 \div 4 = \boxed{8}$ (i) $27 \div 3 = \boxed{9}$

(j) $18 \div 2 = \boxed{9}$ (k) $12 \div 6 = \boxed{2}$ (l) $40 \div 8 = \boxed{5}$

(m) $24 \div 4 = \boxed{6}$ (n) $18 \div 6 = \boxed{3}$ (o) $28 \div 7 = \boxed{4}$

(p) $36 \div 4 = \boxed{9}$ (q) $24 \div 6 = \boxed{4}$ (r) $32 \div 8 = \boxed{4}$

(s) $12 \div 3 = \boxed{4}$ (t) $40 \div 5 = \boxed{8}$ (u) $48 \div 6 = \boxed{8}$

(v) $24 \div 3 = \boxed{8}$ (w) $30 \div 6 = \boxed{5}$ (x) $36 \div 9 = \boxed{4}$

2

(a) $\frac{1}{2}$ of $14 = \boxed{7}$ (b) $\frac{1}{6}$ of $42 = \boxed{7}$

(c) $\frac{1}{4}$ of $36 = \boxed{9}$ (d) $\frac{1}{7}$ of $70 = \boxed{10}$

(e) $\frac{1}{4}$ of $28 = \boxed{7}$ (f) $\frac{1}{7}$ of $28 = \boxed{4}$

(g) $\frac{1}{3}$ of $21 = \boxed{7}$ (h) $\frac{1}{7}$ of $63 = \boxed{9}$

(i) $\frac{1}{3}$ of $60 = \boxed{20}$ (j) $\frac{1}{8}$ of $40 = \boxed{5}$

(k) $\frac{1}{5}$ of $30 = \boxed{6}$ (l) $\frac{1}{8}$ of $48 = \boxed{6}$

(m) $\frac{1}{5}$ of $45 = \boxed{9}$ (n) $\frac{1}{9}$ of $54 = \boxed{6}$

(o) $\frac{1}{6}$ of $24 = \boxed{4}$ (p) $\frac{1}{9}$ of $72 = \boxed{8}$

3

(a) $124 \times 10 = 1240$ (b) $136 \times 10 = 1360$ (c) $209 \times 10 = 2090$ (d) $427 \times 20 = 8540$

(e) $243 \times 40 = 9720$ (f) $164 \times 40 = 6560$ (g) $503 \times 50 = 25150$ (h) $367 \times 60 = 22020$

(i) $58 \times 17 = 986$ (j) $75 \times 19 = 1425$ (k) $136 \times 14 = 1904$ (l) $157 \times 23 = 3611$

Multiplication and division

Facts about x and ÷

3	x	6	=	18
6	x	3	=	18
18	÷	3	=	6
18	÷	6	=	3

7	x	6	=	42
6	x	7	=	42
42	÷	6	=	7
42	÷	7	=	6

1 Write 4 facts (2 of x and 2 of ÷) for each of these:

(a) 12   **(b)** 20   **(c)** 32   **(d)** 48

(e) 35   **(f)** 54   **(g)** 16   **(h)** 56

(i) 30   **(j)** 72   **(k)** 15   **(l)** 45

We want to put the frogs into groups of 6.

6)16

  2 r 4

Answer: 2 groups and remainder of 4.

2 Now do these (3 are done for you).

(a) 7)16   **(b)** 5)13   **(c)** 3)20   **(d)** 5)12   **(e)** 2)19
    2 r2   **2** r3   **6** r2   2 r2   9 r1

(f) 4)25   **(g)** 3)13   **(h)** 3)20   **(i)** 7)25   **(j)** 8)30
    6 r1   4 r1   6 r2   3 r4   3 r6

(k) 5)29   **(l)** 4)35   **(m)** 6)50   **(n)** 6)57   **(o)** 5)49
    5 r4   8 r3   8 r2   9 r3   9 r4

(p) 9)39   **(q)** 7)55   **(r)** 8)66   **(s)** 6)47   **(t)** 7)41
    4 r3   7 r6   8 r2   7 r5   5 r6

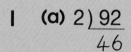
Division

1
  (a) 2$\overline{)92}$ **(b)** 3$\overline{)48}$ **(c)** 3$\overline{)111}$ **(d)** 3$\overline{)165}$ **(e)** 4$\overline{)180}$
      46   16   37   55   45

  (f) 5$\overline{)140}$ **(g)** 5$\overline{)295}$ **(h)** 5$\overline{)785}$ **(i)** 6$\overline{)126}$ **(j)** 6$\overline{)624}$
      28   59   157   21   104

  (k) $\dfrac{2512}{8}$ 314   **(l)** $\dfrac{3060}{5}$ 612   **(m)** $\dfrac{9168}{8}$ 1146   **(n)** $\dfrac{6678}{9}$ 742   **(o)** $\dfrac{5328}{9}$ 592

2 The distance round a square is 1072 metres.
Find the length of each side. $\boxed{268\ metres}$

3

29 of the bananas were not ripe. The rest were put into bags, each holding 8 bananas. How many bags were needed? $\boxed{126}$

4 Estimate the answer first.
  (a) 78 ÷ 13 = $\boxed{6}$ **(b)** 102 ÷ 17 = $\boxed{6}$ **(c)** 144 ÷ 12 = $\boxed{12}$
  (d) 133 ÷ 19 = $\boxed{7}$ **(e)** 105 ÷ 15 = $\boxed{7}$ **(f)** 115 ÷ 23 = $\boxed{5}$

5
  (a) $\overset{15}{23\overline{)345}}$ **(b)** $\overset{16}{17\overline{)272}}$ **(c)** $\overset{22}{24\overline{)528}}$ **(d)** $\overset{24}{23\overline{)552}}$

  (e) $\overset{105\,r22}{38\overline{)4012}}$ **(f)** $\overset{247}{23\overline{)5681}}$ **(g)** $\overset{98}{51\overline{)4998}}$ **(h)** $\overset{185}{37\overline{)6845}}$

  (i) $\overset{92}{72\overline{)6624}}$ **(j)** $\overset{173}{37\overline{)6401}}$ **(k)** $\overset{136}{34\overline{)4624}}$ **(l)** $\overset{73\,r17}{29\overline{)2134}}$

6

This bus holds 76 people.

How many buses are needed to carry 760 people to a pop concert? $\boxed{10}$

Multiples

What are multiples?

The multiples of 2 are numbers that 2 will divide evenly into, such as 2, 4, 6, 8, 10, 12.

Some multiples of 3 are   3, 6, 9, 12, 15, 18.

Some multiples of 5 are   5, 10, 15, 20, 25.

Some multiples of 7 are   7, 14, 21, 28, 35, 42.

Some multiples of 13 are   13, 26, 39, 52, 65, 78.

I

Use a 100 square.

Put a circle round 2 and cross out all the even numbers.

Circle 3 and cross out all multiples of 3. (For example: 6, 9, 12, 14, 15.)

Circle 5 and cross out its multiples.

Circle 7 and cross out its multiples.

1	2	3	4	5	6	7	8	9	10
11	12	13	14	15	16	17	18	19	20
21	22	23	24	25	26	27	28	29	30
31	32	33	34	35	36	37	38	39	40
41	42	43	44	45	46	47	48	49	50
51	52	53	54	55	56	57	58	59	60
61	62	63	64	65	66	67	68	69	70
71	72	73	74	75	76	77	78	79	80
81	82	83	84	85	86	87	88	89	90
91	92	93	94	95	96	97	98	99	100

Circle 11. Why are there are no multiples to cross out? (They have already been crossed out.)

Circle 13. Are there any multiples to cross out? (No)

Circle the remaining numbers which are not crossed out. These numbers can only be divided by themselves or by one. We call these **Prime Numbers**.

List all the prime numbers less than 100.

1, 2, 3, 5, 7, 11, 13, 17, 19, 23, 29, 31, 37, 41, 43, 47, 53, 59, 61, 67, 71, 73, 79, 83, 89, 97

Decimals

 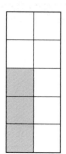

$\frac{1}{10}$ of the pie is shaded.
(0.1 is shaded).

$\frac{9}{10}$ or 0.9 is not shaded.

1 Shaded $= \dfrac{\boxed{7}}{\boxed{10}}$

2 Shaded $= 0.\boxed{7}$

3 Unshaded $= \dfrac{\boxed{3}}{\boxed{10}}$

4 Unshaded $= 0.\boxed{3}$

5 Shaded $= \dfrac{\boxed{3}}{\boxed{10}}$

6 Shaded $= 0.\boxed{3}$

7 Unshaded $= \dfrac{\boxed{7}}{\boxed{10}}$

8 Unshaded $= 0.\boxed{7}$

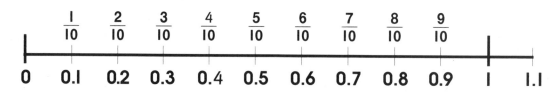

Important facts.

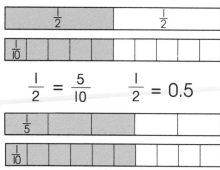

$\frac{1}{2} = \frac{5}{10}$ $\frac{1}{2} = 0.5$

9 $\frac{3}{5} = \dfrac{\boxed{6}}{10}$ $\frac{3}{5} = 0.\boxed{6}$

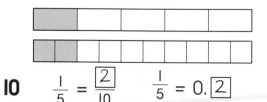

10 $\frac{1}{5} = \dfrac{\boxed{2}}{10}$ $\frac{1}{5} = 0.\boxed{2}$

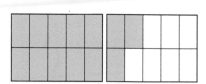

13 tenths are coloured.
1.3 is coloured.

---

11   How many tenths make: **(a)** 1 whole ⑩   **(b)** 3 wholes ㉚

---

12   Write these as decimals:

(a) 17 tenths ⟨1·7⟩   **(b)** 23 tenths ⟨2·3⟩   **(c)** 58 tenths ⟨5·8⟩

(d) 19 tenths ⟨1·9⟩   **(e)** 47 tenths ⟨4·7⟩   **(f)** 60 tenths ⟨6⟩

Basic Rules of Number: Stage 6

Decimals

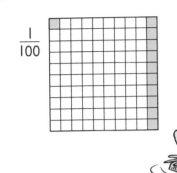
$\frac{1}{100}$

$\frac{1}{100}$ can be written 0.01

$\frac{9}{100}$ can be written 0.09

$\frac{10}{100} = \frac{1}{100} = 0.1$

$\frac{19}{100}$ can be written 0.19

---

1 Write how many hundredths there are in:

(a) 1 whole   **(b)** 2 wholes   **(c)** 5 wholes   **(d)** $1\frac{1}{100}$ **(e)** $2\frac{1}{100}$

    100   200   500   101   201

---

2 Write the following as decimals. (The first is done for you.)

(a) 136 hundredths = $\boxed{1.36}$ **(b)** 204 hundredths = $\boxed{2\cdot04}$

(c) 109 hundredths = $\boxed{1\cdot09}$ **(d)** 106 hundredths = $\boxed{1\cdot06}$

---

3 Write the following in decimal form.

(a) $\frac{56}{100}$ 0·56   **(b)** $1\frac{9}{100}$ 1·09   **(c)** $\frac{80}{100}$ 0·8   **(d)** $2\frac{3}{100}$ 2·03   **(e)** $4\frac{23}{100}$ 4·23

---

4 Insert the correct sign: <, > or = .

(a) 0.2 $\boxed{<}$ 2   **(b)** 0.07 $\boxed{<}$ $2\frac{7}{100}$ **(c)** 10.1 $\boxed{<}$ 11.1

(d) 4.3 $\boxed{>}$ 0.43   **(e)** 0.5 $\boxed{>}$ 0.49   **(f)** $6\frac{1}{2}$ $\boxed{=}$ 6.5

---

5 4.26 can be written $4\frac{2}{10} + \frac{6}{100}$. Write the following in a similar way.

(a) 1.72   **(b)** 3.58   **(c)** 6.04   **(d)** 9.2   **(e)** 7.69   **(f)** 8.27

$1+\frac{7}{10}+\frac{2}{100}$ $3+\frac{5}{10}+\frac{8}{100}$ $6+\frac{4}{100}$ $9+\frac{2}{10}$ $7+\frac{6}{10}+\frac{9}{100}$ $8+\frac{2}{10}+\frac{7}{100}$

---

6 Complete the number sequence.

(a) 2.4, 2.6, 2.8, $\boxed{3.0}$, $\boxed{3.2}$.   **(b)** 6.8, 6.4, 6.0, $\boxed{5.6}$, $\boxed{5.2}$.

(c) 3.1, 3.4, 3.7, $\boxed{4\cdot0}$, $\boxed{4\cdot3}$.   **(d)** 1.2, 2.3, 3.4, $\boxed{4.5}$, $\boxed{5.6}$.

Decimals

More important facts.

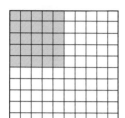

$$\frac{1}{4} = \frac{25}{100} = 0.25$$

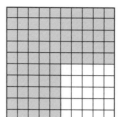

$$\frac{3}{4} = \frac{75}{100} = 0.75$$

1 Find the answer (one has been done for you).

(a) 0.1 of 20 = $\boxed{2}$ (b) 0.5 of 18 = $\boxed{9}$

(c) 0.1 of 60 = $\boxed{6}$ (d) 0.5 of 23 = $\boxed{11\cdot5}$

(e) 0.2 of 80 = $\boxed{16}$ (f) 0.9 of 26 = $\boxed{23\cdot4}$

(g) 0.4 of 20 = $\boxed{8}$ (h) 0.25 of 80 = $\boxed{20}$

(i) 0.4 of 15 = $\boxed{6}$ (j) 0.75 of 40 = $\boxed{30}$

2 Write the following as decimals. (a) $0\cdot012$ (b) $0\cdot071$ (c) $0\cdot087$ (d) $0\cdot106$

(a) $\frac{12}{1000}$ (b) $\frac{71}{1000}$ (c) $\frac{87}{1000}$ (d) $\frac{106}{1000}$ (e) $\frac{563}{1000}$ (e) $0\cdot563$

1.346 can be written: $1 + \frac{3}{10} + \frac{4}{100} + \frac{6}{1000}$.

3 Write the following in a similar way.

(a) 2.648   (b) 4.481   (c) 5.018   (d) 0.156   (e) 1.008

$2+\frac{6}{10}+\frac{4}{100}+\frac{8}{1000}$ $4+\frac{4}{10}+\frac{8}{100}+\frac{1}{1000}$ $5+\frac{1}{100}+\frac{8}{1000}$ $0+\frac{1}{10}+\frac{5}{100}+\frac{6}{1000}$ $1+\frac{8}{1000}$

4 Write the following as decimals.

$$\frac{7}{10} + \frac{3}{100} + \frac{9}{1000} = 0.7 + 0.03 + 0.009 = 0.739$$

(a) $\frac{1}{10} + \frac{9}{100} + \frac{7}{1000}$ = $\boxed{0\cdot197}$ (b) $\frac{0}{10} + \frac{4}{100} + \frac{9}{1000}$ = $\boxed{0\cdot049}$

5 Write these in order, smallest first.

(a) 0.004, 0.044, 0.001 0.4.   0.001, 0.004, 0.044, 0·4

(b) 2.14, 2.414, 2.104, 2.114.   2.104, 2.114, 2·14, 2.414

(c) 6.203, 6.302, 6.023, 6.003.   6.003, 6.023, 6.203, 6.302

Addition and subtraction

When adding and subtracting decimals, the decimal points **MUST** be kept underneath each other.

$$4 + 1.7 + 2.046 + 0.49$$
$$\downarrow$$

```
  4.000
  1.700
  2.046
+ 0.490
-------
  8.236
```

We'll be careful

$$20 - 1.472$$
$$\downarrow$$

```
  20.000
 - 1.472
--------
  18.528
```

1

(a)
```
   2.5
   1.9
 + 3.2
 -----
   7·6
```

(b)
```
   7.6
   3.9
 + 5.8
 -----
  17·3
```

(c)
```
   4.17
   2.93
 + 5.76
 ------
  12·86
```

(d)
```
   8.39
   4.18
 + 6.57
 ------
  19·14
```

(e)
```
   0.9
 - 0.2
 -----
   0·7
```

(f)
```
   0.8
 - 0.3
 -----
   0·5
```

(g)
```
   1.3
 - 0.4
 -----
   0·9
```

(h)
```
   3.5
 - 0.7
 -----
   2·8
```

(i)
```
   7.03
 - 1.046
 ------
  5·984
```

(j)
```
   8.05
 - 2.073
 ------
  5·977
```

(k)
```
   9.12
 - 4.123
 ------
  4·997
```

(l)
```
  10.141
 - 2.517
 -------
  7·624
```

2

Add 2.49 to each of the following numbers.

(a) 7.5   (9·99)
(b) 3.86 (6·35)
(c) 8.6   (11·09)
(d) 4.249 (6·739)

3 Subtract 5.16 from each number.

(a) 10   (4·84)
(b) 7   (1·84)
(c) 20   (14·84)
(d) 9.4   (4·24)

4
(a) $0.9 + 1.8 + 79 =$ 81·7
(b) $1.4 - 1 =$ 0·4
(c) $1.4 + 7 + 3.49 =$ 11·89
(d) $10 - 4.3 =$ 5·7
(e) $2.9 + 3.76 + 3.049 =$ 9·709
(f) $9.1 - 2.04 =$ 7·06
(g) $4.268 + 1.9 + 7 + 29.6 =$ 42·768
(h) $50.2 - 15.23 =$ 34·97

Addition and subtraction

1 How much greater is 43.002 than 21.14? (21·862)

2 How much less is 17.15 than 50.223? (33·073)

3 The sum of three numbers is 15. Two of them are 2.7 and 6.81. What is the third number? (5·49)

4 A rope is 90.55 metres long. Two pieces measuring 27.6m and 29.68m long are cut off. What length of rope is left? (33·27m)

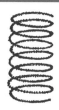

5 A tank of oil holds 300 litres. 17.39 litres leaked out. How many litres were left? (282·61 litres)

6 The total length of the three sides of a flower bed is 12 metres. What is the length of side **(a)**? (3·87m)

(a) 3.27m

4.86m

7 **(a)** 500 − (36.8 + 5.945 + 39.38) = [417·875]

(b) 700 − (146.96 + 58.6 + 89.469) = [404·971]

(c) 800 − (365.84 + 8.7 + 98.26 + 2.598) = [324·602]

8 Round the following numbers to the nearest whole number.

(a) 5.5 (6) **(b)** 3.18 (3) **(c)** 7.619 (8) **(d)** 9.1 (9) **(e)** 20.62 (21)

(f) 25.712 (26) **(g)** 48.499 (48) **(h)** 25.47 (25) **(i)** 22.8 (23) **(j)** 8.007 (8)